BARNVILLE

LET'S GET SOME-THING STRAIGHT.
WHEN FARMER DAVE COMES TO MILK ME, MAKE YOURSELF SCARCE.

YOU'RE LIVING IN A FANTASY WORLD, NELLY. FARMER DAVE DOESN'T KNOW YOU'RE ALIVE...

PLUS, HE'S A HUMAN BEING, HE'S MARRIED, HE'S THE CHURCH PASTOR AND HE'S SECRETLY GAY.

STOP BEING SO NEG-ATIVE, STANLEY. PROM-ISE ME YOU'LL MAKE YOURSELF SCARCE.
OH, ALL RIGHT, I PROMISE.

LATER...
YOU HAVE SUCH WARM HANDS, DAVE.
SICK.

WHAT WAS YOUR NAME AGAIN?
I NEVER KNEW IT COULD BE LIKE THIS.
NELLY, RIGHT?
DIS-GUST-ING.

SEE YOU TOMORROW.
IT'S A DATE!
GAG ME.

STILL THINK I'M LIVING IN A FANTASY WORLD, STANLEY?
GAK!

THE "KVETCH" ABIDES

One panels doomed? Don't be daft, ya git

If a group of crows is a murder, and owls a parliament, around *Bystander* we call any collection of comedy writers a "kvetch." The same, apparently, could be said of one panel cartoonists—on Page 9 there begins a roundtable which is gloomy in the extreme. But who can blame them? We are now fully half a century past the heyday of general interest magazines. and on top of that injury crouches the insult of the internet. While we now know that the Web cannot do what it was invented to do—keep the populace safe and sane in times of catastrophe—it has shown itself to be truly excellent at killing any type of for-profit publishing.

And what about AI? Could it be trained to create one panels? Probably—but I say it's spinach, and I say 10101010.

So you'd think, in our capitalist utopia, where each of us is a rational actor driven by economic self-interest, this would spell a mass exodus from the form. Not so! Thanks to social media, gag cartoons have never been more widely enjoyed, and more people are drawing them than ever. And this too, according to the group, may be a problem. Instead of being driven by jokes, which are hard to think of, time-consuming to execute, and often offend, too many contemporary gagsters aim for a gentle spasm of self-recognition—the pithy depiction of an annoyance or minor social ill that makes the reader think, "Yes. This, too, has happened to me." While few of us have the knack for great jokes, all of us have met someone who can tie a cherry stem into a knot with their tongue.

I genuinely love cartoonists, and adore the modern one panel cartoon, where

MICHAEL GERBER (@mgerber937) is Editor & Publisher of *The American Bystander*.

the joke lies in the interplay between the art and the caption. That delay in perception—the "putting it together" that is required of the reader—turns the whole thing into jazz. At its best, a one-panel can confer a kind of immortality, if only for a generation or two. Such a gem has to be really funny, of course, but also has to be unique to that artist. Sam Gross' "Frog Legs" cartoon couldn't have come from anyone else.

I have a theory—and please note that Sam is no longer here to say, "Ahh, you're full of shit": I think the modern one panel is a profound expression of individuality, and that it—like the modern short humor piece—was born in the wake of World War I. WWI, and later, the Depression, were powerful reminders of the folly of groups; this is why the first crop of one panel geniuses came in the '20s and '30s, followed by a second crop in the '60s and '70s. This second group is passing now, and there is no publishing industry left to nurture a third.

The true geniuses aren't selling "gags." They're presenting a whole worldview, unique to themselves, undrawable by any other hand. Throughout our culture, intense personal expression via mass media is growing rarer. Novelists are no longer central; ditto rock stars. Most of Hollywood's auteurs are from a different era—people like Scorsese and Coppola will not be replaced, any more than Kubrick was. In TV we are hopeful about the strike, but the death of streaming doesn't augur well for the star showrunner. Cartooning is intimate, the product of one unique soul beavering away alone. This is why the recent deaths are so hard—there'll be wonderful cartoons in the future, but no more glimpses into George Booth's world. Or Sam's, or Jack Ziegler's, or Ed Koren's. The lions that are left, people like Mort Gerberg and Sidney Harris, not to mention spring chickens like Roz—I wish them low cholesterol and great health insurance. In the meantime, *Bystander* fights on.

We fight because we will win: Whenever I hear a dire prediction, humor-wise, I think of *The Wipers Times*. Published by British soldiers stationed in the trenches of the Western Front, this humor magazine sprang to life when some Tommies found an abandoned printing press. They decided to publish a journal of war humor, fake ads, cartoons and (this being World War I), poetry. *The Wipers Times*—named after how the Brits pronounced "Ypres"—began in February 1916. It lasted, despite shot and shell and mustard gas and bad poetry—until after the war's end.

If a print humor magazine can survive all that, one panel cartoons can survive a Charles Addams-bot. Lately I've been thinking that the internet itself may not last much longer in its current form; the centrifugal forces it unleashes may be simply too destructive to countries' political systems and societies. There is nothing permanent or inevitable about our current situation, and this era of Tycoons Gone Wild may well be looked on, after its end, as a time of collective madness. Some bad idea we all stumbled into, hoping for the best, never thinking it would get this terrible, something awful that had to run its course. Kind of like World War I.

So let us take a moment to salute the Tommies in the trenches of today, young and old, gamely producing cartoons for our amusement and little remuneration, racking up "likes" and sometimes even immortality (of a decidedly temporary nature). Let us read magazines like this one—and encourage friends and relations to buy subscriptions, *hint hint*—all straining towards the day when peace is declared, heroes are honored, and life returns to normal.

The Pergola des Artistes may have been killed by COVID, but the Tuesday cartoonists' lunch never ends. Ask not for whom the "kvetch" convenes dear reader, it convenes for thee. **B**

Art and Immortality
1952
1978
1980
1992
2006
2007
GALLERY
MUSEUM
ART MOVERS
2026
2052
3001
3052
LC Hansen

TABLE OF CONTENTS

"It sucks, but at least a human did it."

DEPARTMENTS

STATE OF THE ART

A lively discussion on the past, present and future of one-panel carooning featuring Pat Byrnes, Roz Chast, Jason Chatfield, Bob Eckstein, Emily Flake, Peter Kuper, Sarah Morrissette, Oliver Ottitsch, Rich Sparks, Nick Spooner, and others.

FEATURED ARTISTS

The AMERICAN BYSTANDER

Founded 1981 by Brian McConnachie
#26 • Vol. 7, No. 2 • August 2023

EDITOR & PUBLISHER
Michael Gerber
GENERAL MANAGER Laura Fox
HEAD WRITER Brian McConnachie
SENIOR EDITOR Alan Goldberg
ORACLE Steve Young
STAFF LIAR P.S. Mueller
INTREPID TRAVELER Mike Reiss
BIBLE THUMPER Michael Pershan
STAFF ARTISTS Lance Hansen,
Nick Spooner, D. Watson
AGENTS OF THE 2ND BYSTANDER INT'L
Eve Alintuck, Melissa Balmain,
Ron Barrett, Roz Chast, Emily Flake,
James Finn Garner, Rick Geary, Jack
Handey, Pat Kennedy, Jon Plotkin.
MANAGING EDITOR EMERITA
Jennifer Finney Boylan
CONSIGLIERA Kate Powers
COVER BY *D. Watson*

ISSUE CONTRIBUTORS
Marisa Acocella, Lucas Adams, Jeremy Banks, Charlie Barsotti, Jason Bentsman, Andrew Birch, George Booth, David Borchart, M.K. Brown, Pat Byrnes, Jason Chatfield, Tom Chitty, Tyson Cole, Joe Dator, Matt Diffee, Frega DiPerri, Nick Downes, J.C. Duffy, Arun Durvasula, Bob Eckstein, Derek Evernden, Chris Gural, Brandon Hicks, Ed Himelblau, Jeff Hobbs, Lynn Hsu, Michal Jedinák, John Jonik, Michael Johnson, Peter Kuper, Navied Mahdavian, The Surreal McCoy, Steve McGinn, Sarah Morrissette, Paul Noth, John O'Brien, Oliver Ottitsch, Oliver Perry, Jack Reilly, Zach Rhodes, Michael Shaw, Tim Sniffen, Rich Sparks, Peter Steiner.

Lanky Bareikis, Jon Schwarz, Alleen Schultz, Diane Gray, Joe Lopez, Ivanhoe & Gumenick, Greg & Trish Gerber.
NAMEPLATES BY Mark Simonson
ISSUE CREATED BY Michael Gerber

Vol. 7, No. 2. ©2023 Good Cheer LLC, all rights reserved. Produced in tropical storm-kissed Santa Monica, CA, USA.

COMING 10/31/23

LEARN THE DARK ART OF GAG CARTOONING

A CREATIVITY DECK FROM THE NEW YORKER'S EMILY FLAKE WITH PROMPTS, EXERCISES, AND ENCOURAGEMENT

AVAILABLE FROM WHEREVER YOU BUY BOOKS (EVEN AMAZON, IF YOU MUST)

ADDITIONAL CARTOONS BY

Sam Gross, Paul Noth, Jeff Hobbes, Oliver Perry, Arun Durvasula, Steve McGinn, Bob Eckstein, Frega DiPerri, Lucas Adams, Derek Evernden, M.K. Brown, Jeremy Banks, Andrew Birch, Michal Jedinák, Jason Bentsman, Brandon Hicks, Zach Rhodes.

Sam's Spot

"Stick around. He shits in his pants."

COVER

D. WATSON has been drawing great covers since his days at *The Yale Record* back in the late 1950s. When he showed this drawing to me, I immediately knew it had to be a summer cover for *The Bystander*. "Ah," I thought. "I see Don's flown into LAX too."

ACKNO WLEDG MENTS

THE AMERICAN BYSTANDER, Vol. 7, No. 2, (979-8-218-27507-5). Publishes ~4x/year. ©2023 by Good Cheer LLC. No part of this magazine can be reproduced, in whole or in part, by any means, without the written permission of the Publisher. For this and other queries, email Publisher@americanbystander.org, or write: Michael Gerber, Publisher, *The American Bystander*, 1122 Sixth St., #403, Santa Monica, CA 90403. Single copies can be purchased at www.americanbystander.org/store. **Subscribe at www.patreon.com/bystander.** Other info can be found on our website, www.americanbystander. org. Buy Smoking Fish and other merch at our new shop, theamericanbystanderstore.com!

"A spot-on, hilarious look at the absurdities of parenting."

With over 100 wildly-accurate cartoons, this hard-cover collection is a must-have gift for any parent.

You're not a *real* parent until...
by Scott Dooley & Jason Chatfield

Sam navigated perfectly, only by looking at the ground. Age had bent him like a banana, forcing him to face downwards, talking quietly, while the noise of the city was competing with him. While walking through the streets at a turtle-like pace, i had to submit to his banana-like shape, keeping my ears as close as possible to his mouth at all times, not to miss any story, sarcasm or opinionated remark about the superfluous nature of color in gag cartoons.

The american boys must have had a wild time there. Duty, booze and frauleins. One day Sam discovered a magazine or book with french cartoons. Mesmerized by the contend of that object, that day his buddies had to go partying without him. He retreated into study. Not long after, his first book "Cartoons for the GI" emerged.

On another day we had an appointment at the Met Museum. Sam arrived a bit late, after having been to a medical exam. After approaching the cloakroom, a prick on his arm, probably from taking samples, popped up and pretty quickly blood was streaming down his arm... What's so funny about red?

Our meeting point, a side entrance for the old, the disabled and the well informed lazy.

Sam remained cool, while the cloakroom attendant, with panic in his eyes, started to frantically search for a band aid and, much to his own surprise, found one instantly, in what seemed as purely by accident.

Not expecting him to be so generous with his time, i had travelled to New York to maybe once talk to the man, who's work i loved so much and which upon discovering had seemed like a missing puzzle-piece in my education as an apprentice of his artform.

Hanging out at the Met with Sam Gross was educational, not merely in art history, but also business.

Later that day we were at his studio. My English is alright, but occasional gaps in my vocabulary may occur. While going through maps of his collected roughs, not understanding a particular gag, i asked:

Apart from a very mild indication of pity on his face, he seemed to not mind filling the gap.

There would be more to tell, but as you know, life consists of it's limitations. One of those is time...

State of the Art

*We felt the best way to honor Sam Gross was to host a good old-fashioned cartoonists' bitch session.
To encourage Grossian honesty (and liveliness), anonymity was granted whenever requested.
Imagine a long, wine-splashed table—Sam at the head—at the Pergola des Artistes.*

············ ◆ ············

1. ***Do you think 2023 is a good time for one-panel cartoonists? Why or why not?***

"It hasn't been a good time for drawing magazine cartoons since I started a million years ago when magazines started to axe cartoons, one panel or otherwise. Now the problem is even worse as magazines themselves have almost disappeared. The internet is fine in many ways, but the pay sucks." *[Roz Chast]*

"No. The market has dried up too much for it to be an actual 'job.' It is forcing gag cartoonists to split their attention to make a living, resulting in less time being spent honing their craft." *[Anon.]*

"At the risk of being a Debbie Downer, I think 2023 is less than ideal for one-panel cartoonists—but not just for us, it's a bewildering landscape for anyone working in any form of media. Am I envious when I hear the *alterkockers* (check that spelling, I'm a *shiksa*) talk about the old days, when there were scores of magazines to submit to, and *The New Yorker* paid bonuses in cocaine*? Of course I am, but truly I am grateful that I get to do this work at all." *[Emily Flake]*

"Last year, the major gag cartoon markets collectively paid enough money for ten to twelve cartoonists to make a respectable living from it. Maybe twenty, if they lived in low cost-of-living areas. But those revenues were divided among hundreds of cartoonists. And that was last year. This year, more markets are fading. So, from a financial perspective, it is not an ideal time to be a gag cartoonist." *[Pat Byrnes]*

"The amount of people making gag cartooning a viable full-time job has never been smaller. 'Great online opportunities' for gag cartoons? It's near impossible to pay the bills from gag cartooning on that current pay scale, and why should it change? The biggest problem is all the cartoons posted on Instagram is devaluing the brand (granted, there are other factors). Nobody needs to buy a magazine to find a cartoon. One can go online for free. Sometimes we're our own worst enemy." *[Bob Eckstein]*

"The best time to be a one-panel cartoonist is usually while you exist. In that respect: YES." *[Oliver Ottitsch]*

"It will never not be a good time for one-panelists. In fact, it's a great time. As Philip Roth said, 'Satire is moral outrage transformed into comic art.' And there's plenty of outrage to be had these days." *[Nick Spooner]*

"No. Markets have dwindled drastically. (Same for newspaper comic strips, which I also do.)" *[J. Jonik]*

"As far as *The New Yorker* goes, it's a great time for less talented cartoonists, provided they're the right gender and race. But it's a bad time for talented cartoonists of all types because there's less room for you now and no longer a career opportunity no matter how good you are. Ten years ago, I could have named twenty really good cartoonists who regrettably couldn't get into *The New Yorker*. Now, I literally can't name one cartoonist, even the most bang average, who hasn't been in. As a result of that 'progress,' there are twenty truly great cartoonists who no longer bother. There are too many cartoonists now and fewer great ones." *[Anon.]*

"Every time is a good time for cartoons. Hobbes correctly said that life is nasty, brutish and short. Everyone needs to laugh." *[Sarah Morrissette]*

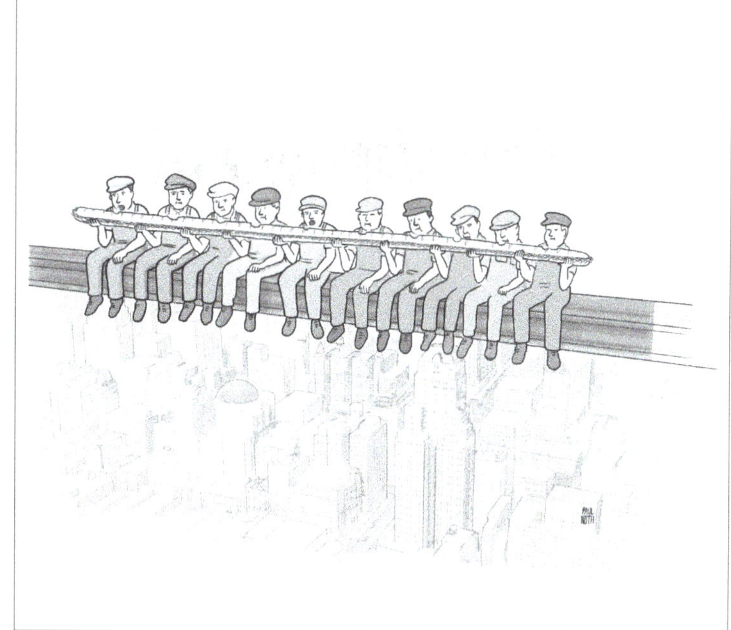

—————
*"Not really, but I hear the office parties used to be *wild*."

2. *Do you think people will be doing this work in twenty years? One hundred years?*

"Twenty, maybe? A hundred, we'll all be too busy hydrofarming or running from sentient AI or eating each other's babies or whatever. Sorry, I don't make the rules." *[Flake]*

"Yes, but not for long. It will never be a lifelong career again, just a hobby or springboard to other things." *[Anon]*

"I certainly hope so but anyone who says they know is lying. Kids don't read magazines. And AI is a real threat." *[Eckstein]*

"Who knows? Maybe it'll come around as some kind of retro nostalgia-bait thing, like *Barbie*, or *Ghostbusters*. If it does take off, it'll be something used more like a meme on a social media platform than a challenging art form worthy of reverence." *[Anon.]*

"No—I think robots will. No idea what people will be doing." *[Chast]*

"If you go backwards, Hogarth was doing it 300 years ago. So, yes." *[Spooner]*

"Assuming we can draw underwater, yes." *[Kuper]*

"Humans make marks on surfaces, and humans have things to say which sometimes subvert the expectations of others. So humans will be creating gag cartoons for as long as they still have the means to express themselves. But they won't get paid to do it unless someone adapts the revenue stream to reward cartoonists for the value they provide. It is in the interest of culture in general to make that adaptation, because the professionalization of art (with the institution of the penny jar at the Globe Theater) brought with it amazing advances in culture. The dilettantism of culture brought on by the internet has diminished both quality and respect for many of the arts. Worse, it has plundered the work of professional artists, depriving them of a livelihood. When artists have to reduce their time creating art, quality naturally suffers. Then the culture suffers." *[Byrnes]*

"Definitely. Cartooning is one of those things that a segment of the population will compulsively do. It's an ancient format that makers and consumers seem to require. The real question is: will there always be outlets where people can find cartoons?" *[Sparks]*

3. *Has the career part of it been what you expected?*

"I never expected to have a career. I thought I'd be living alone in my parents' building living on a government stipend, scrawling my scrawls and eventually descending into mental and emotional chaos." *[Chast]*

"Not really. Whilst I knew it wouldn't last forever, I certainly didn't think it would be so diluted as to become an afterthought. Cartooning could be such a more deeply respected art form if only it held the same attention and respect as fine art. It has always been cheapened by the idea that it's just gossamer. Gossamer has its moments. I'm still going to do it 'til I die. I can't do anything else." *[Anon.]*

"No. I thought I would be creating funny cartoons today, ideally about Trump or global warming, if not to raise awareness, to at least comfort.

But in 2016, *Playboy*, *MAD*, *Barron's*, *Harvard Business Review*, and others, all at pretty much the same time, stopped buying cartoons. I remember hearing from a cartoonist, someone I considered the best cartoonist out there, say to me, 'The party is over. Go home.' That shift ended my career as a gag cartoonist. Up until then it was a full-time job. I had to pivot to teaching, being an art director and publishing cartoon books." *[Eckstein]*

"I always wanted to be a gag cartoonist. As a kid, I would read joke books and try to distill the short anecdotes into gag cartoons. In college, the sound of a pen scratching paper in the silence of the late night was music to me. It still is! I have had opportunities to do many other things and pursue much more lucrative careers. But one thing called to me more compellingly than the others. I believe, in my heart of hearts, that gag cartooning is truly that: my calling. It may strike some as awkward timing that I was called to a profession that is on the skids, but I see it as an opportunity for me to give something back to this art form that has provided me with a lifetime of dreams. A gag cartoon thrives on the unexpected. A gag cartooning career should do no less. None of us know what to expect of the field's future. It is a blank sheet of paper. And who knows better what to make of a blank sheet of paper than gag cartoonists?" *[Byrnes]*

"No. Once things were going well, at

"Hi, welcome to Hooter."

the beginning, I assumed they would continue that way, but they didn't." *[Anon.]*

"Way better. I'm actually making a living and not lying in a gutter as I had anticipated." *[Kuper]*

"'Career'?" *[Spooner]*

"Pretty much, but I thought it would last longer. And I thought *The New Yorker* would always be a standard bearer, a place for the best of the best. I didn't expect it to lower the bar and sacrifice quality for the sake of diversity and inclusion." *[Anon.]*

4. *What are your hopes for the profession?*

"A new wave of practitioners from former third world countries, that hit their societies like a radical punk rock movement." *[Ottitsch]*

"I truly, truly love print media. I love magazines, I hope there continue to be publications that want to buy our little jokes." *[Flake]*

"That more publishers (print or web) pay a lot for good cartoons." *[Anon.]*

"I hope there is a renaissance of single-panel artists who double-down on honing their craft. I hope the quality work leads to finding a new generation of fans that know nothing of the print history of the form, and develop a genuine respect for the creators, the way people followed the world of George Booth or Charles Addams." *[Anon.]*

"There's always hope. This magazine is hope. But I wouldn't call this the Golden Age of Gag Cartooning." *[Eckstein]*

"Survival of the human race so we can continue to draw funny things about being doomed." *[Kuper]*

"I'd love to see it go back to the glory days, but things don't go back." *[Anon.]*

"Cartoons are what sold newspapers and magazines a century or so ago. Cartoons made publishers rich. So publishers took good care of cartoonists. Decades passed, and cartoonists, grown accustomed to this care, came to rely on publishers to keep them and the business strong. When the internet came along, publishers uniformly reacted poorly. They forgot their own business model, which was that subscription costs paid for the paper and ink, and advertising paid for everything else. They threw up paywalls instead of embedding ads in their features and

"Venmo @M-u-g-g-e-r."

sending them forth. In the old days, one person could buy a newspaper, read it, and leave it on a lunch counter for the next customer and the one after that. For the cost of one paper, advertisers could reach three readers. You could leave a magazine on the train, someone else would pick it up, enjoy an article or two, and the advertisers would get what they wanted. Everybody won. We won't get the tangibility and serendipity of printed media back, but we can get a similar kind of revenue model. The technology has been around for a decade or two, at least. Cartoonists used to sell newspapers and magazines not simply because the pictures were pretty or funny. Cartoons capture something integral to the way humans think and help readers think the same way. Cartoonists are valuable to society because of their discipline in seeing things as capable of change and for understanding what is truly happening. Cartoonists are valuable not only to newspapers and magazines, but to the culture as a whole—art, business, society, science, technology, all of it. My hope is to make more people aware of that, cartoonists included!" *[Byrnes]*

5. *Do you have any advice for anyone who wants to do this for a living?*

"Don't do it. Do it as a side thing, if you're driven to, but don't expect to make a living at it." *[Anon.]*

"I'm not in a position to be giving out any advice—I did a bang-up job on my own career and welcome any advice someone has for *me*." *[Eckstein]*

"Wait until I'm dead." *[Ottitsch]*

"Hahahahah. Oh, was that a serious question?" *[Kuper]*

"Remember that the skills you use for gag writing can be applied to many, many other forms of writing and visual art, and develop skills in those disciplines accordingly. Flexibility is key to the freelance life! It also wouldn't hurt to learn a trade. I would have had a lot less panic in my life if I'd gotten an electrician's license or learned to install HVAC." *[Flake]*

"If you're going to do it, take your time to do it properly. Don't half-ass it. Make it your one and only passion, and

"I'll call you back. My kid's about to learn a life lesson."

pay heed to those who came before you, and the lessons they can impart. They're not *all* grumpy bastards." *[Anon.]*

"In the words of Hippocrates, 'First, be funny.' After that, do it because you have to, not because you want to. Bleed in your ink. Work. Hard. Learn to draw, because learning to draw is learning to see. Then learn to draw fast, without thinking. Sketch. Don't 'cartoon,' sketch. Sketch people on the bus or in a park, where you know they'll get up and leave at any moment, so you have to work fast. Sketch for days, weeks, months. Then look back at your sketches. Notice things you had not intended to do, but did repeatedly. For example, 'Why do I keep drawing hands that way? They look better than when I really try.' What you will see is how you see. *Then* do the same thing, except loosen up more by allowing yourself to be less literal, like in a cartoon. Do *not* draw things any particular way because you like a particular cartoon 'style.' Like Roz Chast says, your style should be like your handwriting. It's something you discover when you are not forcing it. As for the ideas, work with what matters to you. If you don't care about the subject, no one else will. Also, an idea is a thought that changes how we see. Changes. Gags that make you say, 'I know, right?' aren't gags. They aren't ideas. They're affirmations.

Memes. Memes have their place, but that place is not in a gag cartoon. This is important to anyone who wants to do this for a living, because if a cartoon idea isn't an *idea*, which transforms the thoughts and vision of others, then there won't be a 'this' to do for a living much longer. Because affirmations, while essential in personal relationships, quickly become vapid in mass communications." *[Byrnes]*

"It will never be a living by itself. Less now than ever before." *[Anon.]*

"Try to draw every day. And; be funny." *[Spooner]*

"There are few publishers willing or able to pay much if anything at all for your really really funny and original cartoons." *[Morrissette]*

6. *Are there any trends you see? Good or bad.*

"Bell-bottoms are coming back. It's good and bad." *[Chast]*

"I feel like I should have a good answer to this! But I don't—I think there is such a wide range of voices working right now that I'd be hard-pressed to pinpoint definite trends." *[Flake]*

"It seems to be more about 'likes' than laughs. You identify a human commonality, then draw someone saying it. You no longer need to make a joke about it. It's about giving people something they can identify with and something they kind of expect. It can even be some-

thing they've already thought or said. They will then give it their thumbs-up and share it with everyone they know. Older cartoons are more about giving the reader something they don't expect, something that surprises them and makes them actually laugh. The social subject matter doesn't matter as much. It's almost like newer cartoons are about figuring out what the reader wants to say and older-style cartoons are more about what the cartoonist wants to say." *[Anon.]*

"There's always been some diversity in gag cartooning. There were Jewish guys *and* Irish guys. In retrospect, these are people from heavily smart-ass cultures. But American culture has become more of a smart-ass culture, and that is increasingly reflected in the faces of cartoonists who look more like America at large. Which is a good thing. I only wish they could look as employed as the rest of America." *[Byrnes]*

"I see a lot of aping of others' styles to try and get 'noticed.' It is a mistake. While you can learn from other artists' stylistic approach, you must never be the second-best anybody. You should aim to be the best you. You should also not all use the same software or process...everyone's line is becoming too indistinct." *[Anon.]*

"Extinction, I believe, is a bad trend." *[Kuper]*

"Less print: bad. More web humour: good." *[Morrissette]*

"Stylistic conformity and compliance with virtue signaling." *[Oliver Ottitsch]*

"In every field there is growth. Science, medicine, whatever. A tennis player today can beat a tennis player from twenty years ago. Baseball pitchers all pitch close to 100 M.P.H. now. I don't see the growth, artistically, in gag cartoons." *[Eckstein]*

"I may be a Luddite, but I hate tablet-rendered cartoons."*[Spooner]*

7. *What do you think is the biggest threat to one-panel cartooning?*

"Two-panel cartoonists. Hate those guys." *[Ottitsch]*

"Political correctness." *[Spooner]*

"Human extinction." *[Kuper]*

"The algorithm. And poor editorial systems. The slashing of budgets in media always cut cartoonists hardest. And first." *[Anon.]*

"*The New Yorker* is bringing in way

too many amateur-level cartoonists and driving away the pros because the pie is now sliced too thin and the prestige is gone." *[Anon.]*

"'Sharing.' Nothing is 'shared' on the internet. Someone is making a buck. If it's not the person doing the work, then it's not 'sharing,' it's plundering. The biggest threat to gag cartooning is the absence of the cartoonist (and often the publisher) from the after-plunder revenue stream." *[Byrnes]*

"The transition going on now is this craft going from vocational to recreational. As a result, the pie has gotten smaller and is being sliced thinner than ever. There are too many people on the stage. Not enough in the audience." *[Eckstein]*

"I would say the dip in quality, but I suspect that readers just get used to dips in quality." *[Anon.]*

8. ***What do you think is the most positive development?***
"Funny pencils." *[Ottitsch]*

"I've been thrilled to see a more diverse group of cartoonists join the ranks—sorely, sorely needed." *[Flake]*

"NFTs have failed. As well they should've. Similarly, digital currency has largely tanked. Blockchain technology is a tool, not an end product. NFTs and bitcoin are like buying and trading wrenches. A wrench is worth nothing unless it has a job to do. Something that blockchain *could* do is keep tabs on how many eyeballs saw a cartoon. Or an article. Or the advertising that sponsored that cartoon or article. Not just how many, but where. So the revenues accrued from those eyeballs could be apportioned fairly. And 'sharing content' could once again become like leaving that newspaper on the lunch counter. Where everybody wins. And cartoonists get paid. News organizations get their old revenues back. They can afford to pay editors and *keep* editors, skilled curators with an investment in getting things right. Which is exactly what the world needs right now." *[Byrnes]*

"The ability to connect with other cartoonists over video calls and chats, to share information. Also the ability to reach our own audiences through subscription services without the need of a magazine or other media publication." *[Anon.]*

"I hear on podcasts cartoonists say it's been a great time for diversity. That would be the one big positive if these newcomers could make a living from it. So *now* we open the doors, now that the cupboards are bare?" *[Eckstein]*

"Digital shareability." *[Spooner]*

"Maybe a positive thing would be the encouragement of work with no words, or implied puns, so that the cartoons would have a global audience." *[Jonik]*

"Lack of extinction." *[Kuper]*

"That *The American Bystander* has found a paying audience." *[Morrissette]*

"Can't think of one." *[Anon.]*

"The possibility that exists now of building your own audience and publishing directly to them." *[Anon.]*

"The diversity of all the newcomers. Not that old white guys haven't done a good job with the form, but it's refreshing to see different takes on standard tropes." *[Sparks]*

9. ***How do you think the work being done today compares to that of the past?***
"Main difference: Fewer three-piece suits worn at the drawing table. A loss, if you ask me." *[Ottitsch]*

"I'm not sure it's a useful comparison—our work reflects our time just as much as earlier cartoons reflected theirs. There are truly gifted draftsmen working now; the aesthetics of today don't always call for the level of craft that was more common in years long past, but also I think we tend to forget that with the exception of those of us who like to really nerd out about this, most people are only familiar with the best of the past—the stuff that stood the test of time. It wasn't all gold in 1947, either." *[Flake]*

"It is considerably worse. I don't entirely blame the artists—who would bother getting brilliant at something they're not getting any work from (other than idiots like me, of course?)" *[Anon.]*

"In the USA the work has become way too 'clean cut.' We're not allowed to joke about anything any more. Cannibals are out. Can I even make a 'Hunchback of Notre Dame' cartoon? Will the hunchbacks of the world hunt me down? Scoliosisly challenged, I mean." *[Morrissette]*

"We lost Michael Crawford, Jack Zeigler, Gahan Wilson, Danny Shanahan, Charles Barsotti, William Hamilton, Al Jaffee, Ed Koren, George Booth, Sam Gross and others in the past few years (just typing this, a flood of emotions are flooding back from the love I had for their work and gratitude for, in some cases, their mentorship and friendship).

That's a good group. We not only lost their work but the competition and inspiration their cartoons generated, directly or even subconsciously like secondhand smoke, a crucial element to cultivating any next wave of artists. Many newbies appreciate their work

"I was born and I died but nothing really got fixed."

The Beautiful Dream

but I know so many new cartoonists I've spoken to (or interviewed on my podcast) are not even aware of these legendary cartoonists…What was the question?" *[Eckstein]*

"The drawing is worse and the jokes are also worse. Too many cartoonists are getting their start in the pages of *The New Yorker* instead of honing their craft for years elsewhere." *[Anon.]*

"Publication size and the time cartoonists can afford to invest in a cartoon (because even a loose and simple drawing can take a long time to get right) make that an unfair comparison." *[Byrnes]*

"A lot more people are doing it." *[Spooner]*

"There do not seem to be single-panelists at the level of Gross, Ziegler, Woodman, Koren, Booth, Addams, and some others." *[Jonik]*

10. *Who are your favorite one-panel people working today?*

"Sam Gross has too recently left the building, to not mention him. Edward Steed. Rudi Hurzlmeier. Has Gary Larson come back yet?" *[Ottitsch]*

"P.C. Vey." *[Anon.]*

"Ed Steed, Will McPhail, and Joe Dator regularly publish work that fills me with envy and despair. And Roz Chast is, of course, my North Star. I have such a wealth of talented peers, seriously pick almost anybody and I will have genuinely admiring things to say about them and their work." *[Flake]*

"Once upon a time, I could afford to have favorites. Now I claim everyone as my favorite, because helping to build a future for them means everything to me. Before I shuffle off this mortal coil, I intend to pitch in and do whatever I can to restore this art form to its rightful place in our culture. Or die trying. That requires me to invest fully in every ally I find on the way. And I see *American Bystander*, and all of its contributors and readers, as allies. Thank you. To the limits of my ability, I got your back." *[Byrnes]*

"Roz Chast, Mick Stevens, Bob Mankoff and Signe Wilkinson are still at it." *[Jonik]*

"Steed, McPhail, and several others who have explored other opportunities than single-panel gag cartooning to share their work with a wider audience." *[Anon.]*

"The usual gang of idiots." *[Kuper]*

"Roz Chast and David Sipress." *[Morrissette]*

"So many of the greats have died recently. I love Rich Sparks' work. I think Tom Cheney is probably the best pound-for-pound cartoonist out there today. I love his stuff." *[Spooner]*

"I don't want to single out one person because there are so many talented, funny cartoonists I'm proud to call my friend."*[Eckstein]*

Sept. 28, 1933 – June 16, 2014

CHARLES BARSOTTI

Like everybody, I've always been a tremendous fan of Charley's work; his widow Rae and daughter Jean are kind enough to send me unpublished drawings for use in the Bystander. Barsotti may be gone, but his cartoons remain wonderful, and his vision of the world refreshing and, to me, oddly hopeful.—MG

"BY GOD, YOU'RE RIGHT~ WE'RE THE WINNERS."

"SEE THAT, GOD?"

"WELL, IF EVERYBODY DOES IT, IT MUST BE O.K."

THE WORLD CUP COMES TO AMERICA
AS GOOD HOSTS WE WOULD DO WELL TO LEARN A THING OR TWO ABOUT IT.
THE HISTORY
SOCCER, OR BASKETBALL AS IT IS KNOWN TO THE REST OF THE WORLD, WAS INVENTED IN 1987 BY ARCHBISHOP ROMOLDO OF MILAN.
ROMOLDO (LATER POPE)
FACT
IN THE INDUSTRIAL NATIONS THE GAME IS PLAYED WITH AN INFLATED BALL.
NFIGLI
SARP
AL
RULES
NEVER APOLOGIZE.
NEVER EXPLAIN.
C Barsotti

PETER STEINER

"I think I was born a cartoonist—I have the constitution for it: loner, watching all the nuttiness from somewhere outside. But I took a detour first, twelve years teaching. And then, after 25 years with The New Yorker *and other publications, I started writing novels, looking for a new adventure. But I still do weekly cartoons for my blog,* Hopeless but not Serious.*"*

GEORGE BOOTH

June 28, 1926 – November 1, 2022

Rule #1 of this job: never throw away anything. When George and I first met in 2016, he sent over a sheaf of roughs he wanted my thoughts on, I printed them out—then the cartoons promptly got swept up in the whirlwind of paper that has been my life since 2015. But I always liked 'em, so I dug them out of my files to share them with you here…and say hello to George one last time.

"Suggest something for dinner.
I've gone empty in the head."

"I bond with things. Now, that I have evolved, I know how not to stand in the way of my future."

BOOTH

In Bystander *since 2023.*

CHRIS GURAL

Born and raised in New York, Chris is a licensed elevator mechanic and a self-taught cartoonist and animator.

"Wood chipper"

"I'm just here for your knees."

"Not exactly."

In Bystander since 2023.

JACK REILLY

"Cartooning isn't all sex, drugs and rock 'n' roll, but it mostly is, if you're doing it right."

"I claim this land for the INVASIVES!"

In Bystander since 2017.

NICK DOWNES

"Cartooning is a profession that offers very long odds on attaining fame & fortune, and very short odds on attaining hours of unacknowledged effort, lots of rejection and a hunched back. Cartoonists, however, at least among those I've known, if given a choice, wouldn't do anything else. I know, I know—it makes no sense."

"Sometimes all it takes is
a little bicarbonate of soda."

"Please tell me we didn't travel 900,000,000 miles for this."

"I don't think he's beached so much as on a break."

In Bystander *since 2017.*

TOM CHITTY

"My son once asked me, 'Daddy, why do you always draw people in little hats, drinking coffee?'"

How long have you been doing one-panels? Did you start as a kid?
I started drawing cartoons in my teens, but with no particular direction. I had a character called "Chew Brain" that I drew on everything. I drew spaceships with silly functions (early versions of the stuff I did for "Your Future House" in *Bystander*).

Do you remember loving any specific cartoonists when you were growing up?
Most of what I read were comic strips. Asterix and Garfield books, then Moomin, Tin-Tin and *Calvin and Hobbes*. I loved a little book called *Zen Comics* by Ioanna Salajan. In terms of single-panel, Gary Larson, of course.

What do you like most about the form? Or dislike?
I'm more naturally suited to triptych cartoons which stretch the definition of single-panel. Traditional gag cartoons are very satisfying to discover because they're harder to find (for me), but that's also the most frustrating part!

Do you feel there's a "typical Chitty cartoon"? Is your style changing?
A typical Chitty is definitely whimsical, and probably a triptych. An example would be "Nonviolent *Clue*," which I did for *The New Yorker*. [The caption reads: "Professor

Plum/In the Library/With a Jolly Good Book."]
The biggest change is that whereas my cartooning and illustration style used to be quite distinct, I now slide between them when there's a good reason..

Is there a "typical Bystander cartoon" for that matter?
A typical *Bystander* cartoon has the whimsy of my single panels, but has a beefier use of illustration. I think of them as "jumbo cartoons."

What's the funniest or most surprising thing a fan has ever said/written to you?
The funniest comments to me are the ones where I've made little mistakes that annoy certain people who are nerdy enough to notice. I once drew a barrel of smuggled violas with six pegs instead of four, in a *New Yorker* cartoon, and the viola police got in touch!

A.V.P.A.B., as the kids say. Speaking of, what do your kids think about your cartoons?
My son once asked me why I always draw people with little hats, drinking coffee.

He'll understand when he has a job—your brain shrinks and you grow very, very tired. You're in Toronto, right?
Correct! Although I was in Derbyshire in the UK until yesterday! That's where I grew up.

—*interview by Michael Gerber*

A draft cover of Tom's upcoming book, to be published by The American Bystander *in 2024.*

Wi-fi at Le Moulin de la Galette

*"No, no, that's a mushroom.
These are bigger and more bready."*

"Fire department, I guess—point is I made too much pasta."

"Can't we go five minutes without you checking your flower?"

In Bystander *since 2023.*

DAVID BORCHART

"Before The New Yorker, *I drew serial stories with ongoing characters. I avoided the single panel cartoon format—in part, I think, because I couldn't imagine how those New Yorker cartoonists came up with all those ideas. Now, after sixteen years in* The New Yorker, *and thousands of submitted cartoons, I'm even more perplexed. How on earth do they do it?"*

"So long, brain cells that remember another Tuesday at Candee's Collectibles."

"I dread turning thirty."

"That guy from the bar—turns out he's an owl. Wait, it gets worse."

"There's the weak link, men—
the Starbucks entrance in the south wall."

"Don't mind them, Red—we liked it."

In Bystander since 2017

LANCE HANSEN

"When I was a kid, I never was into superheroes or anything like that; everything I drew was a knock-off of Don Martin, Jack Davis, Al Jaffee. That's ingrained in my DNA as an artist. My dad was really into my work, but he had died by the time I got into MAD. I kind of wish I'd gotten into that magazine a couple years earlier."

Lance, looking natty.

Do you remember what attracted you initially to The Bystander? Just the fact that there were all these guys involved—I think the first issue even had Terry Jones? A lot of people I wanted to be associated with…and a lot of artists also, I mean, great, great artists. Drew Friedman. At first I was, "It's kind of like *The Lampoon*." But *Bystander*'s really its own thing, which I like, a lot. It's kind of like if you took the cartoons and Shouts and Murmurs, and got rid of all the long articles that you never finish out of *The New Yorker*. But *Bystander*'s not only highbrow, there's some more lowbrow stuff that snuck in too. I love the magazine.

What attracts you to bringing high art and low art into conversation?

One of my biggest influences is Ivan Brunetti, and he's done a lot of that sort of stuff—biography, comics—about various intellectuals. The fourth issue of his comic *Schizo* was a total game-changer for me; he started delving into these real people, and doing it in this comic way. Brunetti had sort of pared down his style a lot, and as a result, I started to simplify my own style.

I see a lot of books about artists—graphic novels or whatever—and they're drawn in a style more suited for superhero-type material…To me, simple art just resonates a little more strongly. It's like Sergio Aragonés; he can convey so much with no words. There's something about pantomime that really, really gets me, and it's kind of the same thing with the more cartoony style.

For example, my John Kennedy Toole piece [*in Bystander #25*]: the tragic events of Toole's life are set up as jokes. Having them rendered realistically would be horrible. I don't think it would work at all.

We also might pay attention to different things, right? I could imagine paying attention to the details, whereas your more abstract, cartoonish form allows you to draw attention to the contours of his life.

Can we talk about the cover for Bystander #25? Where did the cover come from?

When Michael asked me to do it, I was shocked. In the very beginning of this year, I wrote a list of things I wanted to accomplish, and one was to pitch a cover for you guys—not having any clue that he would ever ask me. It's been a murderer's row of great artists who have done the covers, up until then, up until #25.

Including #25!

Stuff by these people who I really admire. So when he asked me, I was shocked. He asked me to pitch a couple ideas, so I just started brainstorming and sketching it out.

My other idea was going to be, some people laying on the hood of a car and looking up at constellations, but with made-up constellations in the sky.

But I wanted to do dancing. It's springtime…I think there's a Jules Feiffer cartoon with a girl dancing, and it's an ode to spring or something. I don't know. But maybe that's where it comes from. But I liked the idea of dancing.

I drew two little kids looking in the window. My daughter Louisa is the redhead, and then my other one, Dolly, is wearing the hat.

The color that I first sent were a lot more like *Peanuts* kind of colors. Real bright, which I don't usually do. But then I brought it down to what I would usually do, and it worked a lot better—Hal's Dance Studio is a rundown kind of place.

What makes it apt for The Bystander?

Kind of sad, kind of sweet, but not saccharine. I didn't want it to seem cynical. I wanted it to have a kind of a sweetness to it.

You have some longer projects you're working on, right?

I have a book out in September, illustrated limericks called *Limerature 101*. They're all based on books; I started doing them while I was just staring off into space at work.

I'm also illustrating *Art is a Weapon*, a life of the anti-Nazi satirist and collagist John Hartfield. I'm working on it with his grandson.

—interview by Michael Pershan.
The full version appeared on our Substack. Subscribe at www.theamericanbystander.substack.com.

*"I think what I'm really looking for is a Darcy
in the streets and a Wickham in the sheets."*

"Just think of the exposure."

B

NAVIED MAHDAVIAN

In Bystander since 2018.

Before becoming a cartoonist, he received his M.Ed. from Stanford University and taught the 5th grade, where he learned most of his jokes.

"Sure, they're magic beans, but you still had to water it."

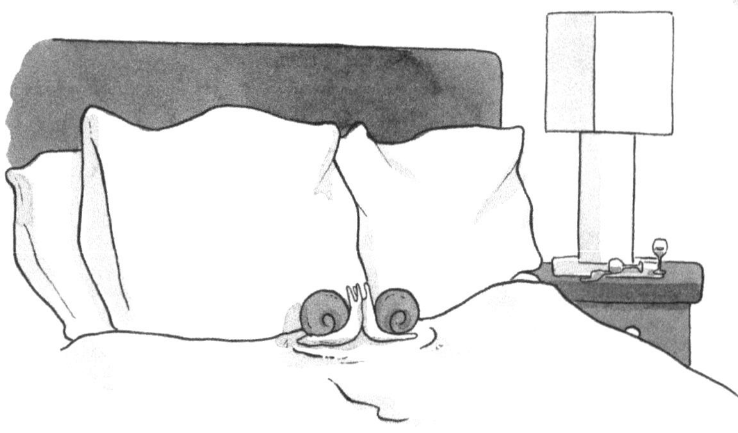

"I'mmmmmmmcartommmmmmmmmmmmmmm coooooooooooooooooooooooooooooooom…"

In Bystander *since 2023.*

PAT BYRNES

"I wanted to be a cartoonist since before I knew you could do that for a living. I studied aerospace engineering just to go to a school that had a daily paper where I could draw cartoons."

"POOF. DISAPPEARED."

In Bystander *since 2017.*

NICK SPOONER

"I heard Sam Gross didn't dislike my work, which nearly made me lactate with pleasure."

NICK SPOONER *before…*

How long have you been doing gag cartoons? Did you start as a kid?

I know for a fact I drew my first one-panel at five, because my sweet, supportive father framed it, and I've enclosed it here. It wasn't the slightest bit funny, but the backwards writing indicates severe, undiagnosed dyslexia, which explains a lot.

Do you remember reading any specific cartoonists when you were growing up?

Of course, and they are legion. The standouts from my pre-teen years were Don Martin, Sergio Aragonés and Antonio Prohías from *MAD*, Johnny Hart (*BC* and *The Wizard of Id*), Charles Addams and the delightfully insane B. Kliban, who was a huge influence. When I discovered my older brother's issues of *National Lampoon*, Sam Gross, Gahan Wilson and Shary Flenniken (whom I would like to thank for my first pubescent "stirrings") were the standouts. And in high school, Garry Trudeau (who cartooned for the same high school paper I eventually drew for), Gary Larson and Bill Watterson.

What do you like most about the form? What do you dislike?

I'm at my happiest when I'm drawing, particularly when I nail the exact facial expression or body posture I'm going after. What I dislike is that I'm not a natural—it takes me a long time to get one gag right and drawn to my satisfaction. Hands continue to bedevil me.

Do you feel there's a "typical Spooner cartoon"? Is your style changing?

I don't know that I've drawn enough cartoons to declare a "typical Spooner," but what I'm going for is "bent." Or even better, "sick." I think there's a thread of that throughout my efforts. As for a "style," it's definitely still a work-in-progress.

Is there a "typical Bystander cartoon" for that matter?

IMHO, Most of what I've seen is "Lampoonesque," which I adore. If *New Yorker* cartoonists are the popular kids, the *Bystander* artists are the misfits cutting class and smoking reefers out behind the gymnasium.

What's the funniest or most surprising thing a fan has ever said/written to you?

I heard Sam Gross didn't dislike my work, which nearly made me lactate with pleasure. I know for a fact that a certain *Simpsons* head writer said one of my recent pieces was "the funniest cartoon he's seen in twenty years," which blew me away. And tripled my lactation flow.

Understandably. Which cartoon was it?

"Zombie Jesus" from *Bystander* #24.

What do your kids think about your cartoons?

I don't share all of them with my offspring, but for those I do they usually smile and say, "Don't you dare post that on social media."

…and after.

"'Jury of my peers'—what a joke!"

"Honestly, Morton! We're on in three minutes!"

"I don't give a rat's ass if they're ants!
We need a fourth for cribbage."

"No, son…how about we walk down there and eat 'em all?"

ED HIMELBLAU

In Bystander *since 2023.*

"I began drawing cartoons as a counter to my day job as a scientist. Inspired by New Yorker cartoonists, especially Chast and Booth, I started drawing single-panel gags about people working in labs. (I have a free newsletter devoted to science and lab cartoons: sign up at www.himelblau.com)."

"So Janet asked if we wanted to meet up sometime and…
Jesus! This guy is right on our ass."

In Bystander since 2021.

LYNN HSU

"After twenty long years of working as an architect, my path veered from drafting straight lines to sketching more playful ones. Now I enjoy writing funny, twisted stories and drawing cartoons in Boston. Check out my work here: @loopyline (Instagram) and lynnihsu.com."

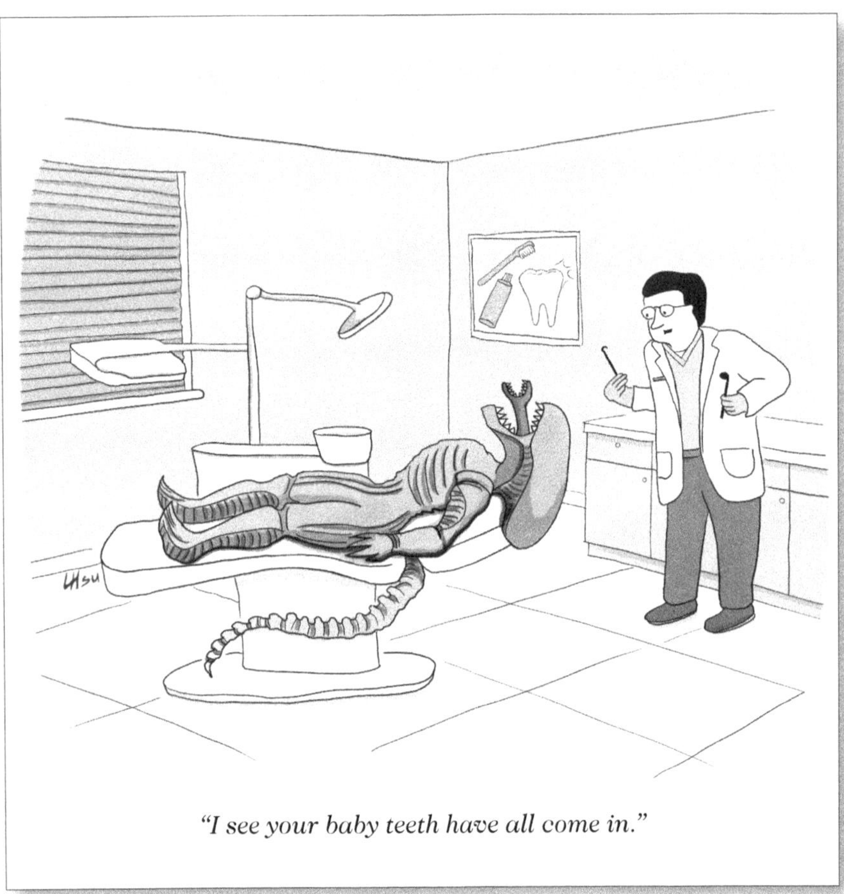

"I see your baby teeth have all come in."

"Your greatest symphonies will be immortalized in carpet cleaning and dog food commercials."

"Your story would have been better at 2x speed."

"Just relax and hold still."

In Bystander *since 2016.*

RICH SPARKS

"I am the child of nudists. You haven't experienced true heartbreak until your drunken Uncle Carl accidentally drags his penis through your birthday cake. You haven't endured real mortification until your college girlfriend sits eating at a TV tray next to your naked, shaved parents. And unless your dad left his ballprints in the newly poured concrete patio, you have led a charmed and frictionless life. So yeah, I'm a cartoonist."

ECHO CANYON
SPARKS

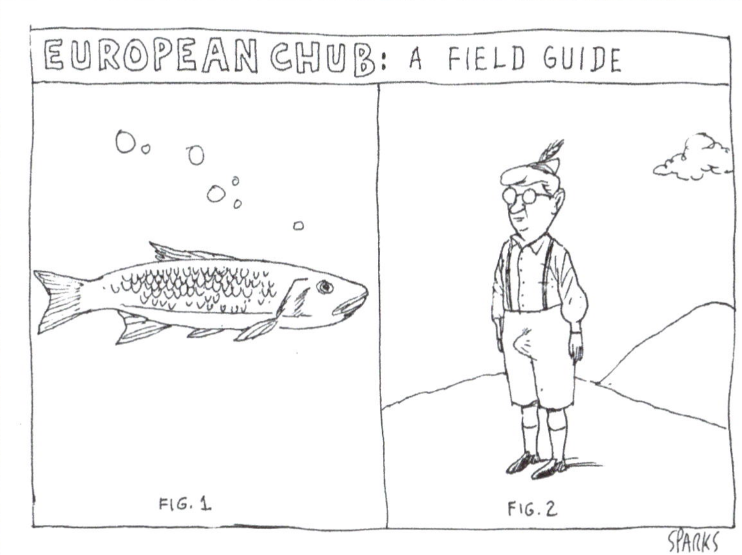

EUROPEAN CHUB: A FIELD GUIDE
FIG. 1
FIG. 2
SPARKS

NUDE DESCENDING A STAIRCASE
SPARKS

The Village Thumb
SPARKS

JOHN JONIK

In Bystander *since 2016.*

"I have been drawing cartoons since Catholic grade school, when sketches of nuns with guns holding us kids as prisoners were a hit...except with the nuns."

"I won't be long. I'm just going around to Spike's for a few beers with my ilk."

"Keep an eye on him, Lou. I'll contact the sign department."

In Bystander *since 2023.*

MARISA ACOCELLA

"I've drawn fabulous women with fabulous shoes since I was 3. Why? My mother was a shoe designer. (She designed Jackie Kennedy's shoes.) But when I was 8, they bored me. The women didn't speak! That is, until a family vacation in a dilapidated Bermuda house that hung drawings with captions on its walls. It was James Thurber's house!"

"A little transparency would be nice."

"I told him I would only have sex with someone I love who could raise the kundalini with me, slowly opening all the seven chakras until the energy goes upwards, then release it into the Universe—that's how I got rid of him."

"Want to watch the government tell the government they're going to save us from the government?"

In Bystander *since 2023.*

JASON CHATFIELD

"Every time I've broken the news to a young artist that they're a 'Born Cartoonist,' I hasten to add that it feels more like a diagnosis than a compliment—and there's no cure! A true cartoonist is compulsively scribbling, ceaselessly contorting their worldly experiences into ideas that might make a good gag, wasting reams of paper to get just the right expression…Cartoonists don't draw because they can, they do it because they can't not."

"*Now who's being naive, Diane?*"

"*Unsubscribe?*"

"*I should start a podcast.*"

Frega DiPerri

Jeff Hobbs

A Bouquet of Wildfowers

"Well, this is me."

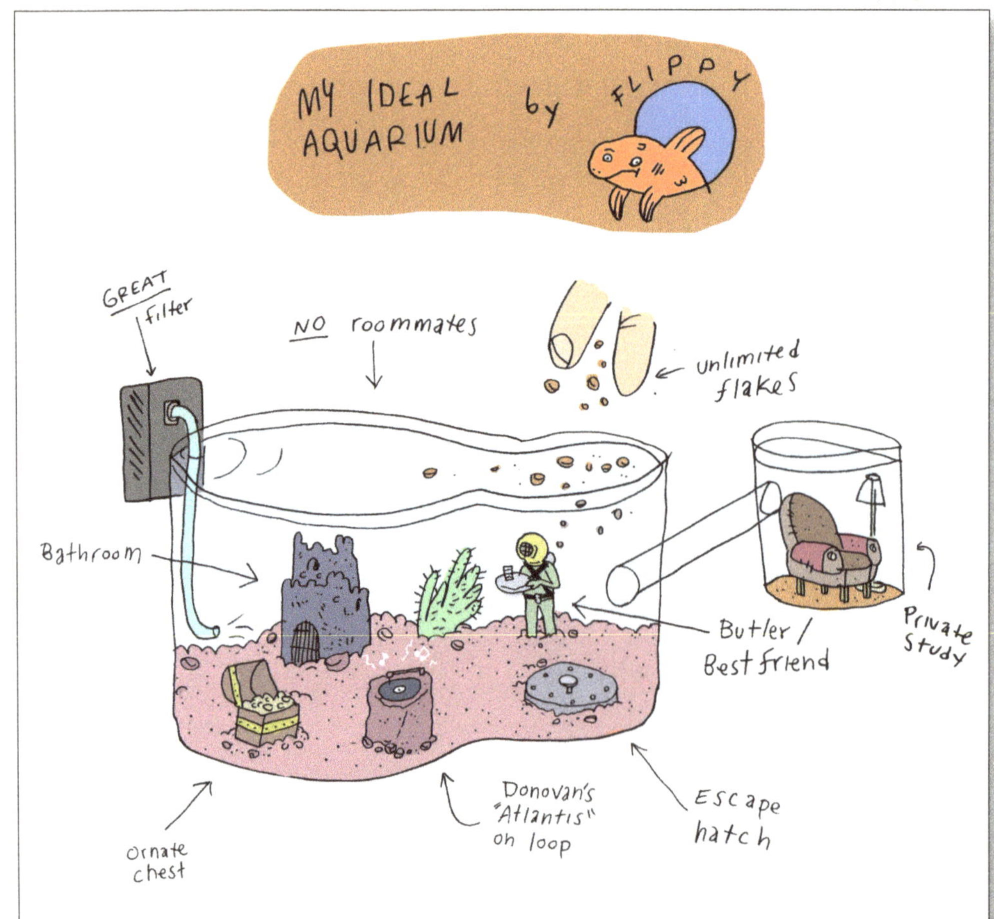

Lucas Adams

Derek Evernden

M.K. Brown

Jeremy Banks

Andrew Birch

Michal Jedinak

Jason Bentsman

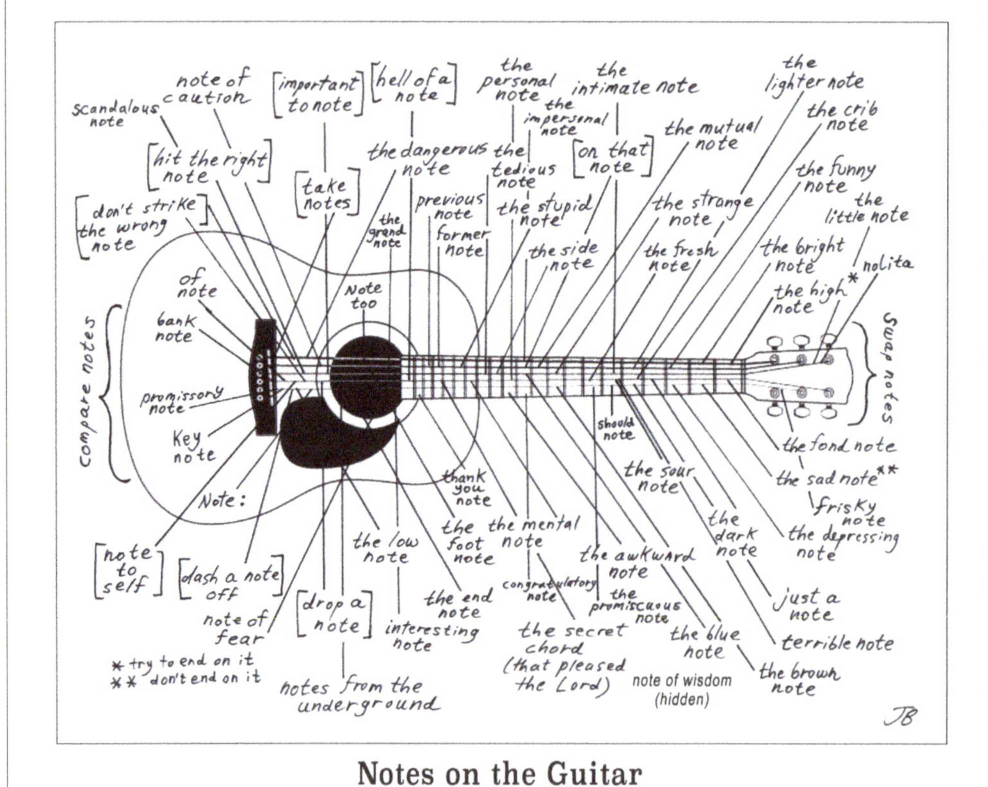

Notes on the Guitar

FROG RACING
A Memory By Brandon Hicks

WHEN I WAS A KID, I USED TO RACE FROGS.

FIRST, I'D HAVE TO CATCH ONE IN THE POND BY MY GRANDPARENTS'S CAMP.

THIS WAS A CHALLENGE, BECAUSE THE FROG NEEDED TO BE FAST ENOUGH TO WIN A RACE, BUT SLOW ENOUGH TO BE CAUGHT BY A 6-YEAR-OLD.

AH-HA!!
RIBBIT!

WHEN I HAD THE FROG, I'D TRY TO MAKE IT AS COMFORTABLE AS POSSIBLE BY CONSTRUCTING A LITTLE "HOME" FOR IT.

KRAFT™ PEANUT BUTTER JAR
AIR HOLES
TWIG
GRASS & LEAVES
A DRAWING FOR COMPANY

I'D THEN BE TAKEN DOWN TO THE DOUGLAS HARBOUR FIRE STATION WHERE THE RACES WERE HELD.

MY MEMORY IS FUZZY, BUT I RECALL THE RACES AS BEING GRAND, WELL-POPULATED EVENTS. IN RETROSPECT, THIS SEEMS UNLIKELY.
RACES!

MY FROG NEVER WON, BUT I WAS NO LESS PROUD.
I DON'T CARE. YOU'RE STILL THE BEST ONE.

I DOUBT THAT THEY DO IT ANYMORE, AND THEY PROBABLY SHOULDN'T, BUT IT WAS A GREAT EXPERIENCE FOR A KID.

BRANDON HICKS

Zack Rhodes

AN UNEXPECTED GENDER REVEAL PARTY

In Bystander *since 2023.*

MATT DIFFEE

"What I like best about being a gag cartoonist is the moment I come up with an idea. When an idea comes together, I get the same little jolt of discovery or recognition that the reader gets later. It's actually better for me, because it comes with a surge of relief after fighting the fear I'll never have another idea ever again."

"Watch out for that one. They call her Dances With Crabs."

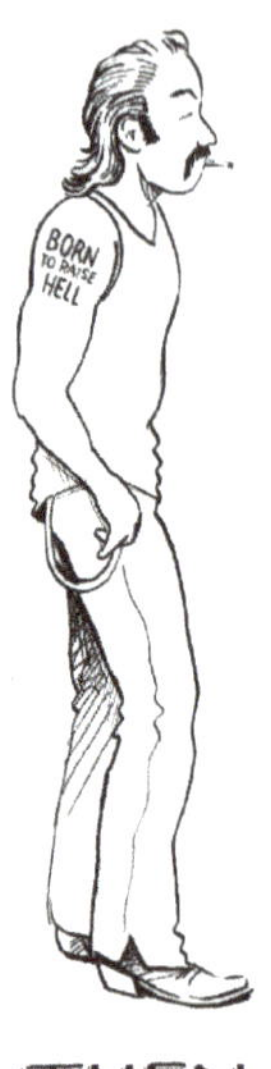

"How's the lumbar support?"

*"A little advice, make sure the image is
in the public domain."*

"Hey Buddy, my eyes are down here."

"Gesundheit."

In Bystander *since 2019.*

OLIVER OTTITSCH

"I have been drawing cartoons and funny comics—or trying to—since a youthful discovery of a MAD paperback in a shop near my elementary school in Austria. My first cartoon collection in English is called Gay Nazi Dolphins at a Gang Bang."

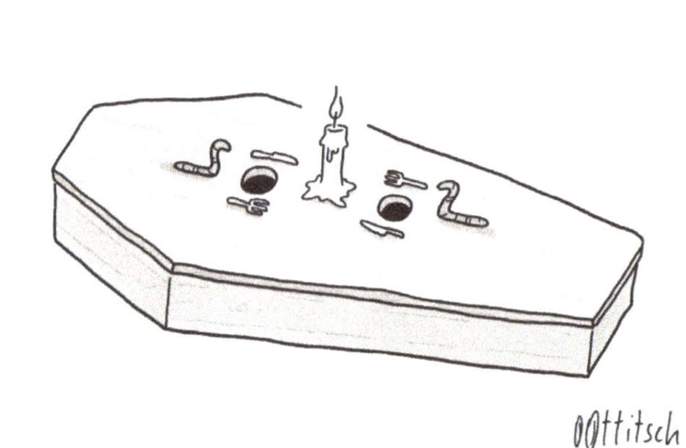

In Bystander *since 2016.*

PETER KUPER

"Peter wanted to be an entomologist until he saw a Spiderman comic (age 7) and switched careers. He now splits his time between the two disciplines, by making comics about insects. His graphic novel INterSECTS will be published in the Spring of 2025 assuming we survive the next election cycle and planetary meltdown."

" Would you prefer Cool Mint, Creme Brulee, or Mango ?"

"Hold up! According to Scopes, this is a myth!"

EMILY FLAKE

Emily got her start with an alt-weekly strip called Lulu Eightball; she is now somehow a frequent contributor to The New Yorker. Emily's latest book is a creativity deck about gag cartooning called Joke in A Box. She is the founder of the St. Nell's Humor Writing Residency for women and non-binary humor creators in Williamsport, PA. In the middle of all this activity, Emily lives in Brooklyn with her husband, daughter, and disquietingly large cat.

"Ew, Burning Man isn't cool—
my parents met there."

"Yeah, well, maybe next time don't give us genitals!"

"Thank you for your recent submission. However,
we feel the market for desert island cartoons…"

In Bystander *since 2018.*

BOB ECKSTEIN

In addition to being an ace cartoonist and humorist, Bob is also the world's foremost expert on the snowman. "I found the first ever drawing of one. It's in the margins of an illuminated manuscript—a book of hours from 1380. The greatest sculptors in the world were commissioned to make snowmen. Michelangelo made one for the Pope."

"...and if re-elected..."

"He died doing what he loved—making people laugh."

BOB ECKSTEIN's office/ship captain's quarters,
Washington Heights, NY.

In Bystander since 2017.

JOE DATOR

"People often ask me the secret to cartooning. It's to always draw from your true life experience. I carry a notebook everywhere, and if something funny happens, I write it down. Every one of the cartoons you see here actually happened to me. If nothing funny ever happens to you, then you are not funny, and you can't be a cartoonist. Sorry."

"You'll never have to worry about bedbugs if you just get some bed scorpions."

"No, I'm his brother Boozo."

*"This track is for victory laps only.
The defeat lap track is over there."*

*"Excuse me, we were having a private conversation
about being hot and thirsty."*

"Never mind, it's just a shampoo unicorn."

TIM SNIFFEN

In Bystander *since 2023.*

"As of this printing, the O'Malley girl has not yet been found. See more work at timsniffen.com or wherever malcontent teens lean on windowsills, looking towards the sunset and plotting their escape to a city big enough to hold all their dreams."

In Bystander *since 2023.*

THE SURREAL McCOY

The Surreal McCoy (UK). Cartoonist. As seen in The New Yorker, Sunday Times, Private Eye *and other unlikely places. First graphic memoir* The Wolf of Baghdad *published by Myriad Editions, one of* The Guardian's *top graphic novels.*

THE TOUR OF FRANCE BEFORE THE INVENTION OF THE WHEEL

In Bystander *since 2022.*

SARAH MORRISSETTE

Like so many of the best one-panel cartoonists, Sarah is also an excellent illustrator. When I saw these watercolors she did of Victorian circus performers, I was mesmerized and knew I had to slot them into the issue. Enjoy—and let us take a moment to celebrate the exquisite versatility displayed by today's so-called "gag cartoonists."—**MG**

S
M
2012

In Bystander *since 2023.*

MICHAEL SHAW

"If I were to choose from the Big (recently-ish) Dead Three of Barsotti, Booth and Gross, I would come down squarely in the Gross camp. I don't really consider my humor 'sick,' just a bit mean-spirited, crotchety and squarely staring the slack-jawed horror of our existence squarely in the ear. My ethos has always been 'Tragedy plus time, equals humor. But who has time anymore?' And for we, the rapidly ripening, that becomes truer every day."

"You're adopted."

"He wanted to see who fingered him."

*"What really grinds my gears is that by this time next year,
I'll look exactly like you."*

"Eating those always gives you the shits."

In Bystander *since 2022.*

MICHAEL JOHNSON

"All of these cartoons are based in reality. They are actual events that I witnessed with my own eyes. In fact, they're not even cartoons, they're photographs. Photographs of real, living people."

"Houston, we've made a gross oversight,
and morale is at an all-time low."

"Yes, a second Metro line would benefit our city's commuters,
but at the risk of introducing a vexing ethical dilemma."

"When I asked for notes and feedback
I was only looking for praise and flattery."

subj: trading my soul for crossbow
to: god
cc: jesus
bcc: satan

"Sorry for oversharing, but you're such a friendly bench."

"They desperately want me to be a lion and
I don't have the heart to tell them I'm a coat hanger."

"But enough about me,
tell me some of your sins."

"Sure, the abyss is great for staring into.
But if screaming is your thing, you'll want to go with the void.."

In Bystander *since 1981*

ROZ CHAST

"I had to make up my own way of making cartoons. A friend of mine has a kid who is an artist. The mom is an artist, too. Sometimes my friend would try to show her kid a more efficient, better way of doing something, and her kid would say, No, I want to do it the child way. I completely identify with that."

PARTICLE POEMS

A wave and particle drove to town
In a beautiful pea-green bus.
A boson cried, "I have no ride,"
And the wave said, "Come with us."

There once was a foolish neutrino
Who went to a Vegas casino.
He got into debt
While playing roulette,
His luck was no better with keno.

As I was walking in the park
I stepped upon a tiny quark.
I got scared and ran away
And that was what I did today.

In my grandma's candy dish
Are lemon drops and muons
And lots of Werther caramels
And sour balls and gluons.

John OBrien